Fix Your Credit in Six Easy Steps

Fix Your Credit in Six Easy Steps

For Less Than $50

THE SMITH GROUP

To order additional copies of this book, contact:
Xlibris Corporation
1-888-795-4274
www.Xlibris.com
Orders@Xlibris.com
67827

Contents

FOREWORD

CREDIT IS A very important asset to have in our society. The practice of having good credit and maintaining excellent credit is even more important. If you are like me and millions of other people all over the world, you may have had credit problems. Many people have had credit problems that keep them from obtaining the things they want or need in this society.

Having bad or negative credit is not the end of the world. After reading this book, you will be able not only to fix your credit in a few easy and very inexpensive steps but to manage it as well. **Credit fixing** is the legal activity of correcting errors contained on any or all of the three consumer credit bureaus – TransUnion, Equifax, and Experian – which warehouse consumer credit information.

THIS IS NOT A MAGIC PILL!

The highly complex nature of storing every American citizen's credit history over the course of no less than ten to twelve years leaves much room for mistakes, errors, and even false information.

Credit fixing has been made easier for the average consumer, and more difficult to sell as a service because of federal regulations.

Typically, any consumer who writes a letter disputing any inaccurate information can expect to have such information deleted from their credit bureau after having sent two such disputes by mail or over the Internet.

The wording of these letters, and the persistence required to correct any disputed information, is where professional services are employed.

Credit fixing services are like hiring someone to do your taxes, except tax laws are much more complicated and filing requires much more record keeping. Many of the services, which send too many disputes in order to overload the computer systems of the credit bureaus in order to remove accurate information (derogatory or otherwise), have a temporary effect on your actual credit report and operate in a quasi-legal manner.

Credit bureaus have free Internet Web sites where every consumer may access their credit report and send in disputes.

Credit repair occurs after all information contained on a report is updated and accurate, time is allowed for derogatory information to "heal," and new credit being paid on time is granted to the consumer.

Retrieved from http://en.wikipedia.org/wiki/Credit_fixing.

PREFACE

THIS BOOK IS dedicated to the millions of people who suffer from bad or adverse credit. There are many books on consumer credit, credit counseling, legal aspects of credit management, and many other credit repair topics. This book will prove you do not have to be burdened by negative credit ratings and you can have the houses, automobiles, merchandise, credit cards, and cash that you dream of having in this society. This is a must-have book for any college student, family, single family, and anyone who purchases merchandise in this society.

This effort is dedicated to my parents, family, and friends, past and present, who believed in me and helped me through the good times and bad. This manual would not be possible if it were not for the love, friendship, guidance, and training received throughout the years. The most important quote that I feel would be appropriate for this book is to always remember that "your dreams are as real as you are prepared to make them" (Sidney Poitier).

ABOUT THIS BOOK

THE PURPOSE OF this book is to help anyone who has a negative impact on their credit report. Many people have negative credit status, and this prohibits consumers from achieving the things vital to the pursuit of happiness. This book is for anyone who is thinking about fixing and maintaining his or her credit status.

This manual is for people like me, who have problems in life such as life itself. No one person is immune to bad things happening to them. No one is immune to bad things such as bad timing of financial and emotional events in your life or just plain bad luck as we call it. Things happen that are beyond our control and sometimes beyond the realm of understanding.

This book can and will show you how bad luck, bad timing, and bad decisions do not have to leave you in a negative situation. This book is designed for people such as mothers, fathers, students, teachers, hairstylists, military personnel, single parents, divorced, married, separated, low income, high income, slow learners (like myself), and shopaholics. This manual is for people who are new to the United States and all people who work shop and purchase anything in this country.

I hope to capture everyone as this book is for you, and if I have left anyone out, please understand this book is definitely for you as well. By the end of this book, you will be able to find out what is on your credit report, define it, understand it, fix and maintain it, and get this, it will only cost pennies – that's right, pennies. This book offers insight on how to obtain a credit report, FREE, and how to monitor it and maintain a good credit score and clean the report for your own benefit.

My staff and I have researched each section of this process and have found this way to be the easy, cheap, and fastest way to clean your credit. This book has a glossary of common credit terms that are used in deciding your credit score and reporting on your report. This manual offers the six-step process on how easy it will be to start taking care of your credit report.

This manual will show you how to monitor and maintain the report status and keep your credit standing at a good score level. The book will inform you about certain myths versus facts associated with credit repair and credit monitoring.

This credit repair manual will fix the following items on your credit report:

Identity theft

Charge-offs

Collection accounts

Write-offs

Late payments

Liens

Bankruptcies (certain types)

Repossessions

Judgments

CHAPTER 1

Here Is How It Works

THE GOVERNMENT ASSIGNS scores and a rating to the credit status of each individual. This score determines what we can purchase and what kind of finance rate and credit limit we can have. A credit score is a "credit rating that represents an estimate of an individual's financial creditworthiness as calculated by a statistical model. A credit score attempts to quantify the likelihood that a prospective borrower will fail to repay a loan or other credit obligation satisfactorily over a specified period of time. A credit score is typically based on the information in an individual's credit report."

Lenders such as financial institutions, credit card companies, and department stores use credit scores to manage and mitigate the risk posed by lending money to consumers (Wikipedia, credit score, 2006). Note that initially, the credit score was first considered a "beacon score," which indicates a score from a particular agency such as Equifax. It is now consolidated and considered a credit score. The better the score, the lower the finance rate; this equates into more resources that can be purchased by an individual. Since the term "more is better" was coined, people have been trying to purchase as many items as they can or cannot afford. Having good credit assists with this method of purchasing.

The next procedure is for a company to assign an individual credit rating to your account request. A credit rating measures creditworthiness, the ability to pay back a loan, and affects the interest rate applied to loans. ("A company that issues credit scores for individual credit-worthiness is generally called a credit bureau or consumer credit reporting agency." [Wikipedia, credit rating agency, 2006])

Negative items on your credit report can prohibit you from making the purchases you may need or desire. Bad credit can stay on a consumer's credit report for seven to ten years. The ways to clean up your credit will be defined in this book. This book will explore and explain the factors that decide what score and ratings are assigned and how the credit is determined in this society. From the reading of this material, you will be able to manage your credit as well as clean up your negative credit in six easy and simple steps.

CHAPTER 2

Definition of Credit

C REDIT IS DEFINED as a monetary term, refers to the granting of a loan and the creation of debt. Any movement of monetary funds is normally quite dependent on credit, which in turn is dependent on the reputation or creditworthiness of the entity, which takes responsibility for the funds (Wikipedia, credit, 2006).

What this means is since the end of the barter system in which merchandise was traded for or purchased with merchandise, people and companies have done business by offering credit to buyers. This process makes it possible for people to purchase without cash or other merchandise such as fruits, animals (yes, farm animals), furniture, and other items.

The credit process is very important to a company's revenue or bottom line. Good management of the credit policy helps companies maintain revenue and collect more cash over time; this process keeps companies in business and keeps profits growing at a higher, faster rate.

Definition of Credit Scores and Ratings

Personal Credit Ratings

In countries such as the United States, consumers are assigned a credit score by companies called "credit bureaus." In the United States, this is a three-digit number known as the **FICO credit score**. The concept of these scores started back in

1956 with two men named Bill Fair and Earl Isaac. Fair was a mathematician, and Isaac was an engineer. They funded the Fair Isaac Company, now known as FICO score.

> The system today is standardized the way the financial industry extends credit to individuals. One's credit score, along with the credit report, affects one's ability to borrow money through financial institutions such as banks and credit cards. In Canada, the most common ratings are the North American Standard Account Ratings, also known as the "R" ratings, which have a range between R0 and R9. R0 refers to a new account; R1 refers to on-time payments; R9 refers to bad-debt. The factors which may influence your credit rating are: ability to pay a loan, interest, amount of credit used, spending money instead of using it for useful purposes e.g. paying back a loan, saving patterns, spending patterns and many more. (Wikipedia, 2006)

Range of Scores

A FICO score generally ranges from 300 to 850. It exhibits a left-to-right reading with a national average of 725 points. The score of 660 is generally regarded as potentially low and represent an important break point for creditworthiness. The performance of the scores is monitored, and the scores are periodically aligned so that a credit grantor normally does not need to be concerned about which scorecard was employed.

Each individual actually has three credit scores for any given scoring model because the three credit agencies hold their own independent databases. These databases are independent of each other and may contain entirely different data. Many lenders will check an applicant's score from each bureau and use the median score to determine the applicant's creditworthiness.

A new VantageScore has been offered by all three credit bureaus to creditors since spring 2006. It will soon be available to debtors. Its range is from 501 to 950. It is graded A (901-950), B (801-900), C (701-800), D (601-700), and F (501-600). It remains to be seen whether the VantageScore will replace the FICO score or even be accepted by many creditors (Wikipedia, 2006). (***Great, now that we are done with the boring stuff, let's get to the fun stuff!***)

Introduction to the Process

As a consumer in this country, I have seen good times and, unfortunately, bad times. Each experience helped me in many ways, as I am always told that you have to take the bad along with the good. Well, folks, this statement does not apply to "credit ratings." I eventually found out that having bad credit does not help anyone.

Millions of Americans suffer from the effect of negative credit status; this makes it very difficult to obtain credit and purchase the things you want or possibly need. This book will assist you in the search for that good credit status and help you maintain that status as long as you apply the important principles listed in this book. This book is valuable to everyone – and that includes students, adults, rich, poor, and any race, creed, or culture that does business in this country. Everyone can benefit from having good credit, and this book will show you how to obtain and keep it.

CHAPTER 3

Myths versus Facts

Myth: Once an individual reaches "negative credit" or "bad credit" status, you can never achieve a good credit rating.

Fact: *Proper credit monitoring, maintenance, along with credit repair, can assist all individuals with getting the credit back on track and in good standing in the financial community. Example: A credit monitoring system, either online or conducted by the individual, can prevent negative items from appearing on your credit report.*

Myth: It takes seven to ten years to repair bad credit.

Fact: *Most credit bureaus will remove any negative item per the law and at the specific request of the individual. The credit bureaus have forty-five days to investigate and remove negative items from the report that cannot be verified. The average time for cleaning credit is normally thirty days. This book will show you how it is done. Example: Upon observing negative items on his report, the author disputed each item and attached the statute that permits the credit bureaus to investigate and eventually remove the items that were deemed negative. This process took thirty days or less. The statute is Public Law 91-508, called the Fair Credit Reporting Act.*

Myth: A low credit and beacon score can be final and often financially fatal and can be passed on to family members.

Fact: *The credit bureaus have the job of maintaining a report for each individual separately. No one can be penalized for any other family member's negative items; these can be investigated and removed by law. Example: At one point in time in the author's life, the author noticed a few items on the credit report that were not incurred by him. He contacted the bureaus by the methods to be shown and had the items removed.*

Myth: **Credit companies, agencies, credit repair firms, law offices, and others are the only entities that can fix or repair credit.**

Fact: *This is one of the biggest myths about the credit repair process. There are many companies that advertise these services; however, this is only a myth. By LAW, no one can repair a credit but the individual themselves. Example: The three major credit bureaus will only respond to the request of the individual. Each agency that advertises this credit repair service will ask you to supply them with a credit report, which you have to request on your own.*

They will only supply you with the letters (which we will show you how to obtain) then mail the letters to the credit bureaus. They will charge the consumer for the services that they themselves have not done.

The credit bureaus investigate the issues then only report back to the individual. So-called credit repair agencies know this. They prey on the consumer's inability to recognize they are doing the work themselves. The agencies are useful in many ways, however not when it comes to credit repair. This is a process that can only be completed by the consumer.

Myth: **Repairing credit can be a long and painstaking process.**

Fact: *In this book, we will show you how fast this process can occur. The credit repair can be fixed in no time at all. Most cases, in one month, the consumer is on their way to having more purchasing power and will be able to get products and services at lower interest rates.*

Example: A few short weeks after applying the principles outlined in this book, the writer began to receive multiple correspondences in the mail for credit cards at lower rates, home and car refinancing information, and many other perks that come to those who have good credit.

Myth: **The credit bureaus will not cooperate with me.**

Fact: *The credit bureaus are bound by law to assist, investigate, and remove all negative items from your report in a timely fashion. They have to cooperate with the consumer; it is the law of the land. Example: There is the Public Law 91-508 called the Fair Credit Reporting Act.*

Myth: I do not have the time to manage and monitor my credit report.

Fact: *Bad credit and identity theft occurs at a very fast rate. People can't afford NOT to manage THEIR credit report. It is every person's obligation to manage their own report monthly. This book will outline such a process.*

Myth: It is very expensive to receive a credit report.

Fact: *Getting a credit report is easier and cheaper than ever before. You do not have to pay high prices for the report; it can be given to the consumer for free. That's right, FREE of charge. This book will show you how it is done.*

Myth: "Only credit agencies can negotiate my credit standing, they are trained in such matters."

Fact: *This myth is a huge misconception. The agencies work for YOU, in conjunction with YOU, and they can only do what YOU tell them to do. The CREDIT BUREAUS only respond to the request of the consumer; no one can intercede on your behalf. This process exists to protect the consumer from identity and fraudulent individuals who prey on unsuspecting consumers.*

Myth: Having good credit is only for the rich.

Fact: *Anyone can fall victim to negative credit, and that means rich people and poor people alike. Repairing credit is a luxury that everyone can afford because it is neither costly nor time-consuming. This book will show you how inexpensive it really is to clean up your credit.*

Myth: I cannot monitor my own credit report.

Fact: *Anyone can monitor his/her credit report. Each individual can subscribe to a credit monitoring service or simply check the status of his/her report monthly, quarterly, semiannually, or yearly (most offer free credit reports and scores, which are a plus). This is done by simply staying in contact with the credit bureaus and making arrangements to view your report when you purchase new items or establish new credit.*

Myth: "Debt consolidation" procedures can clean my credit.

Fact: *Debt consolidation only serves to combine each debt into one payment. The consolidation results in a substantial monthly payment. Credit is not repaired or cleaned* *until the final payment is received, and even then, debtors are not obligated to remove anything from your report. The consumer will still have to dispute the paid items in order to get them cleared off the report.*

Myth: Bad credit cannot be removed.

Fact: *Bad credit can be removed and deleted in two ways: One of which is when a time occurs that the item is deemed not economical to pursue. This normally occurs in about seven to ten years. The other way to have an item removed is the way shown in this book. Disputing an item per the law permits the credit bureaus to investigate on your behalf.*

The credit bureaus send a request to the debtors requesting any information that bears a signature of the requestor or individual attempting to repair credit. The company has thirty days to reply to the bureaus with the information. If they do not reply, the item is removed from the report and your score increases, thus granting more purchasing power for the individual. This works! THIS IS WHAT THE GOVERNMENT DOES NOT WANT YOU TO KNOW!

Myth: Paying off past due balances removes them from my credit report.

Fact: *Paying off past due amounts does NOT guarantee a removal from the credit report. The credit bureaus are not obligated to remove any items unless the ten-year time limit has occurred or the individual specifically requests the item be removed. Once an old item is paid off, the bureau is only obligated to show the item as being paid and also paid late – this is not good for credit scores.*

Myth: Having good credit offsets the bad credit on my report.

Fact: *Having good credit is always a plus; however, companies such as finance companies, auto agencies, mortgage realtors, furniture stores, etc., can hold negative items against the buyer. The more there are negative items on the report, the more you would have to explain or justify the financial status to a lender – this could mean being financed at a higher interest rate or not being financed at all.*

Myth: Items that have been removed can sometimes show up on my report again.

Fact: *Once an item is investigated and eventually removed, it NORMALLY will never show up on your report again. The credit bureaus investigate each item, and once it is discovered, the item does not belong on your report. The item is permanently removed from the report.*

CHAPTER 4

Step-by-step Methodology of Cleaning Your Credit

1. *The first step in credit repair is to order your credit report.* This can be done for FREE – yes, FREE. Here's how: consumers (***this means anyone who purchases merchandise in this country***) – each consumer can receive a free copy of their credit report once a year from the three national credit agencies, which are Equifax, Experian, and TransUnion.

   Consumers from all across the country and other areas can go to www.annualcreditreport.com and freecreditreport.com and contact them at 877-322-8228. (***This is not a paid advertisement for annual report or free credit report sites.***) The consumer should give them your social security number or contact them by mail at Annual Credit Report Request Service, Post Office Box 105281, Atlanta, GA 30348-5281. Consumers may expect an instant response by e-mail and a two-week time period by mail. There are a few other ways to get a free consumer credit report.
   You are entitled to a free report if YOU call 877-322-8228, which is the central center and will give you all three reports free of charge!

   - You reside in Colorado, Georgia, Maine, Maryland, Massachusetts, New Jersey, or Vermont.
   - A person has taken action against you due to information on your credit report.

- You are or believe you have been a victim of identity theft and have placed a fraud alert on your credit report (this is very important and highly recommended – it will be in the next edition to the series, called maintaining your report and credit status).
- You believe your credit file contains inaccurate and erroneous information as a result of a fraud on your report.
- You are on public assistance (welfare, social security, Medicare, etc.).
- You are unemployed and expect to file unemployment within the next sixty or so days.

The next few pages show examples of the Web sites.

Exhibit A: AnnualCreditReport.com

Note: This is one of the Web sites to utilize for your free credit report.

Exhibit B: Freecreditreport.com

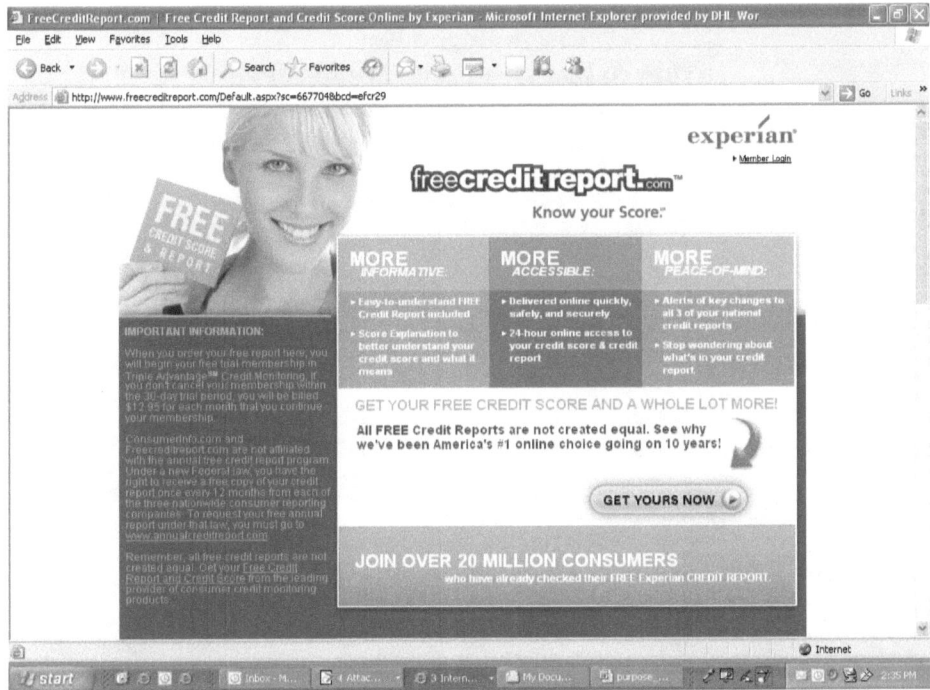

2. *The next step in the process is to review your credit report.* This can be done by simply ordering it from the credit bureaus like the ones listed above (annualcreditreport. com) and (freecreditreport.com). Here is a sample of how this should appear when it has been received.

Exhibit C: Example of Credit Report

Credit Report Key
How to Use This Credit Report Key
First, check to see that your account and personal information is correct. Then to understand each section, please refer to the corresponding numbered explanations below.

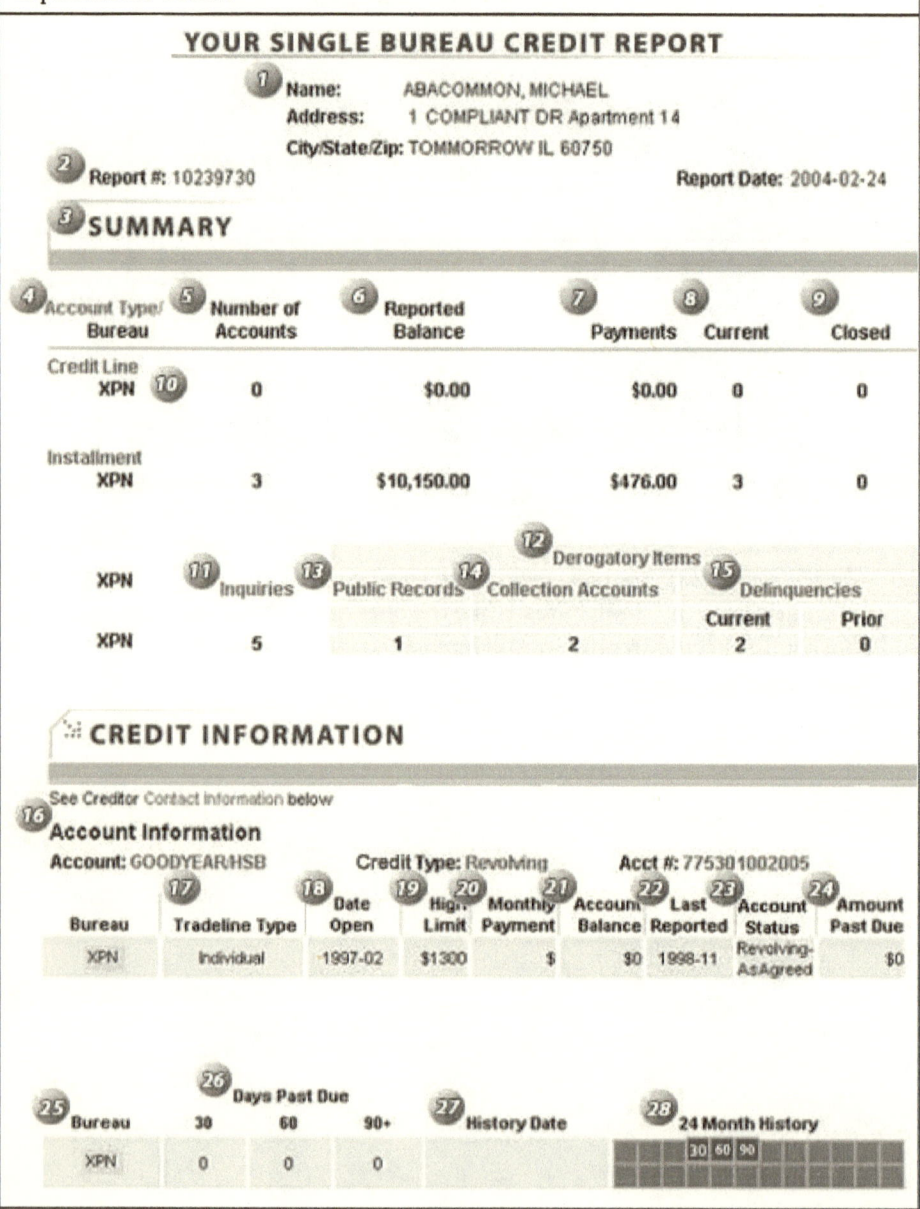

YOUR SINGLE BUREAU CREDIT REPORT

Name: ABACOMMON, MICHAEL
Address: 1 COMPLIANT DR Apartment 14
City/State/Zip: TOMMORROW IL 60750

Report #: 10239730
Report Date: 2004-02-24

SUMMARY

Account Type/ Bureau	Number of Accounts	Reported Balance		Payments	Current	Closed
Credit Line XPN	0	$0.00		$0.00	0	0
Installment XPN	3	$10,150.00		$476.00	3	0

	Inquiries	Public Records	Collection Accounts	Derogatory Items Delinquencies		
XPN					Current	Prior
XPN	5	1	2		2	0

CREDIT INFORMATION

See Creditor Contact Information below

Account Information

Account: GOODYEAR/HSB   **Credit Type:** Revolving   **Acct #:** 775301002005

Bureau	Tradeline Type	Date Open	High/ Limit	Monthly Payment	Account Balance	Last Reported	Account Status	Amount Past Due
XPN	Individual	1997-02	$1300	$	$0	1998-11	Revolving-AsAgreed	$0

Bureau	Days Past Due 30	60	90+	History Date	24 Month History
XPN	0	0	0		30 60 90

CREDIT REPORT KEY

1. Personal Information
Check to see that your name, current address, and date of birth are correct.

2. Report Number
Refer to this number when making inquiries.

3. Report Summary
Sums up current credit accounts and balances, and notes delinquent or overdue amounts.

4. Account Type
Shows the type of account (credit line, installment, mortgage, open, revolving).

5. Number of Accounts
Shows the total number of accounts reported for each type of account.

6. Reported Balance
Shows the total balance of all types of accounts.

7. Payment
Shows the sum of payments for each account type.

8. Current
Shows the total number of current accounts.

9. Closed
Shows the total number of accounts reported closed.

10. Credit Bureau
Indicates which of the three main credit reporting agencies (Equifax, Experian, and TransUnion) reported the information.

11. Inquiries
Shows the total number of inquiries about your credit that were reported. (Inquiries may be made by banks, department stores, employers, and landlords.)

12. Derogatory Items
Shows the delinquent/derogatory information that has been reported by the credit reporting agencies.

13. Public Records
Shows the number of matters of public record (court records of bankruptcies, tax liens, judgments or foreclosures, etc.) reported by the credit reporting agency.

14. Collection Accounts
Shows the number of accounts turned over to a collection agent, as reported by the credit reporting agency.

15. Delinquencies
Shows the number of accounts that are currently delinquent or derogatory, or were previously delinquent or derogatory.

16. Account Information
Refers to the creditor with whom you have or had an account with, the account number, and type of account.

17. Trade-line Type
Explains who is responsible for the account and the type of participation you have with the account.
A: Individual Account, Z: Authorized User, C: Comaker, U: Undesignated, J: Joint Account, S: Spouse's Account, M: Maker, and T: Terminated

18. Date Open
Indicates when the account was opened.

19. High Limit
Indicates your credit limit, or the most you have ever charged on the account.

20. Monthly Payment
Refers to your monthly payment for this account.

21. Account Balance
Refers to the balance you owe, as of the date the information was obtained.

22. Last Reported
Refers to the last date the account was updated by the creditor.

23. Account Status
Indicates whether the account is current or past due.

24. Amount Past Due
Shows the total past due amount for all accounts.

25. Credit Bureau

Indicates which of the three main credit reporting agencies (Equifax, Experian, and TransUnion) reported the information.

26. Days Past Due 30/60/90

Indicates that any balance that is past due will appear in the Past Due 30/60/90 amount columns. Past Due 30/60/90 indicates the number of times an account was overdue thirty, sixty, or ninety days within the past seven years.

27. History Date

Refers to the date at which current history begins.

28. Twenty-four-month History

For chronological reference. Indicates whether the account was current or past due on a month-to-month basis over the last twenty-four months and 151, including the date shown under "History Date."

▮ Not reported that month		OK Current Account	
NB Current Account No Balance		TN Too new to rate; approved but not used	
30 30 days late		60 60 days late	
90 90 days late		120 120 days late	
150 150 days late		CO Collection or charge-off	
WB Wage earner plan or bankruptcy		RF Repossession or foreclosure	

3. *Step number 3 consists of the credit letters to use to repair your credit.* This is done by simply using the letters in this book for your purpose. There are three agencies and, thus, three letters to use that will clear your credit. At this point, you are on your way to a brighter financial future. The letters below should be sent to TransUnion, Experian, and Equifax. The addresses are as follows:

> Experian: 701 Experian Parkway Allen, Texas 75013
> Equifax/CSC: P.O. Box 981221, El Paso Texas 79998-1221
> TransUnion: P.O. Box 1000 Chester, PA 19022

Next step: Insert the addresses and agencies in the fields that require the agency name – one letter works for all three requests.

Sample Letter

Mr./Mrs. Customer (Your Name)
XXXX Lakeside Estates Dr. #XXXX (Your Address)
Houston TX 77042

TransUnion (Selected Credit Agency)
P.O. Box 1000 (Agency Address)
Chester PA 19022

Today's Date

Dear TransUnion (Agency Name):

This letter serves as a formal complaint that you are reporting inaccurate credit information.

I am distressed and disturbed that you have included in my credit profile the information below and have failed to maintain reasonable procedures in your operations to assure maximum possible accuracy in the credit reports you publish.

Credit reporting laws confirm that credit bureaus can only report 100% accurate credit information. Every step must be taken to assure the information reported is completely accurate and correct.

I request a reinvestigation of the following information. I also respectfully request to be provided proof of these alleged items, specifically the contract, note, or other instrument bearing my signature. Failing that, these items must be deleted from my credit report as soon as possible.

(INSERT NEGATIVE ITEMS FROM REPORT HERE)
MERC ADJ BUR, acct. XXX
ATTN L.L.C., acct. ABCDE
CRDT MGT, acct. XXXX

The listed items are a very serious error in reporting; they are completely inaccurate. Please delete this misleading information, and supply a corrected credit profile to all creditors who have received a copy within the last six months or the last two years for employment purposes.

Additionally, please provide me with the name, address, and telephone number of each credit grantor or other subscriber.

Under federal law Public Law 91-508, you have thirty days to complete your reinvestigation. Also, I request the description of the **exact procedure(s)**, including but not limited to **contact name, telephone number, fax number, e-mail address, etc., of the person providing the information** used to determine the accuracy and completeness of my information, which is to be provided within fifteen days of the completion of your reinvestigation.

Sincerely,

Mr./Mrs. Customer
MY SSN: XXX-XX-XXXX

Review the letters to be sent.

These letters should show the negative items in the center of the page for the credit investigator to investigate and respond to you. Once the letters are complete with negative items in the center, print, review, and prepare for mailing.

4. *The next step is to proceed to the post office to get the certified and return receipts for mailing the letters. Here is a sample of the certified and return receipts for mailing.*

Exhibit D: Certified Mail Receipt for Mailing
(Fee [in addition to postage] = $2.40)

U.S. Postal Service
CERTIFIED MAIL RECEIPT
(Domestic Mail Only; No Insurance Coverage Provided)

Postage $

Certified Fee

Return Receipt Fee
(Endorsement Required)

Restricted Delivery Fee
(Endorsement Required)

Postmark
Here

Total Postage & Fees $

Recipient's Name (Please Print Clearly; to be completed by mailer)

Street, Apt. No.; or PO Box No.

City, State, ZIP+4

PS Form 3800, February 2000   See Reverse for Instructions

Instructions for Completing the US Postal Service – Certified Mail Receipt

1. Fill in recipient's name and address at the bottom of form, and your department name and zip in the area above the postage box.
2. DO NOT fill in postage and fees, the post office will do this for you and return the receipt to your address. If you do not need the postage and fees portion filled in, you may tear off and keep your receipt.
3. Peel backing from the bar-coded label and place at the top of the envelope immediately to the right of the return address so the dotted line is even with the top of the envelope. Fold the upper green part of the label over the top of the envelope.
4. Send to post office for delivery.
5. Please dispose of old certified labels that do not have a bar code on them. The post office will no longer accept forms without the bar code.

Exhibit E: Return Receipt for Mailing (Cost = $1.85)

SENDER: COMPLETE THIS SECTION	COMPLETE THIS SECTION ON DELIVERY	
■ Complete items 1, 2, and 3. Also complete item 4 if Restricted Delivery is desired. ■ Print your name and address on the reverse so that we can return the card to you. ■ Attach this card to the back of the mailpiece, or on the front if space permits.	A. Signature X	☐ Agent ☐ Addressee
	B. Received by (Printed Name)	C. Date of Delivery
1. Article Addressed to:	D. Is delivery address different from item 1? ☐ Yes If YES, enter delivery address below: ☐ No	**(Front)**
	3. Service Type ☐ Certified Mail ☐ Express Mail ☐ Registered ☐ Return Receipt for Merchandise ☐ Insured Mail ☐ C.O.D.	
	4. Restricted Delivery? (Extra Fee) ☐ Yes	
2. Article Number (Transfer from service label)		

PS Form 3811, August 2001   Domestic Return Receipt   102595-01-M-2509

UNITED STATES POSTAL SERVICE   ‖‖‖   First-Class Mail
Postage & Fees Paid
USPS
Permit No. G-10

• Sender: Please print your name, address, and ZIP+4 in this box •

(Back)

The return receipt is used to accompany a Certified Mail receipt or an insured mail piece. The recipient signs the return receipt, and it is sent back to the sender for proof of delivery.

1. Return receipt MUST be sent as certified, registered, insured, or express mail.
2. Complete items (1) address to, (2) article number, and (3) service type. Also, complete item 4 if restricted delivery is desired.
3. Print YOUR name and address on the reverse so your card will be returned to you.
4. Attach the card to the back of the mail piece, or on the front if there is enough space.
5. Send to post office for delivery.

Exhibit E: Sample Envelope (Cost = 39¢)

UNITED STATES POSTAL SERVICE
STAMPED ENVELOPE UNIT
Printed Stamped Envelopes Made To Order
Phone (814) 832-3496
PO Box 500
Williamsburg. PA 16693-0500

——— Sample ——— **29** USA

Love

5. *Instructions are as follows:*

1. Write sender's name and address at the top left corner of the envelope.
2. Write name of credit bureau agency in center of envelope.
3. Enclose credit letter inside envelope, seal, and affix certified sticker on top center of envelope. Affix return receipt on back center of envelope after envelope is sealed. Now your envelope with credit request for investigation letter is ready to be mailed.

6. *Now comes the fun part. After the credit bureaus receive your letters, they will then investigate the claims by contacting each creditor and demanding they send proof of a signed contract with your signature on the document.* **Identity theft victims should be especially interested in this portion of the process as the negative items that are not signed by the claimant will be investigated and removed for lack of proof.** Note: *The great part is the credit bureaus may not have the information with your signature attached (especially if it is not signed by you and someone has tried to steal your identity). This is a legal process, and this will ensure your request for credit removal on your report is complete.*

In about two weeks after mailing the letters, you will receive a letter from the credit bureaus notifying you they are investigating your claim. At this point, ALL INVESTIGATED ENTRIES will be removed from your report. *Most credit repair companies tell you this is the way they can save your credit, it is NOT.* The best is yet to come. The letter can take many forms, but here is a sample of how it will look to you.

Sample Credit Letter

From: Experian/TransUnion/Equifax Credit Bureau
To: Mr./Mrs. Consumer
We have received your request for the investigation on the following accounts:

> Acct – XXX
> Acct-YYY
> Acct – ZZZ

We are currently investigating the accuracy of each account and will be in contact with you at the completion of the investigation. The results of the investigation will come in the form of a letter indicating the investigated inquiry has been removed from your account or the inquiry will remain on your credit report.

Regards,
Credit Bureau Representative

In about two more weeks or so after mailing the letters, you will receive a letter from the credit bureaus notifying you they are investigating your claim. At this point, ALL INVESTIGATED ENTRIES will be removed from your report permanently! The final letter has a few different forms; however, the letter should closely resemble the sample on the following page:

Date of this report DD/MM/YYYY Did you find and error on your CSC credit file?
CSC Credit Services Dispute online at www.csccredit.com
PO Box 619054
Dallas TX 75261-9054 If you do not have Internet access, mail disputes.
CSC Credit Services-Disputes

Consumer Name
Consumer Address
City, State, Zip Code

Please find enclosed the results of your request for CSC to reinvestigate certain elements of your CSC credit file. Our investigation has now been completed.

Trade-line Information
ACCOUNT NAME – ACCOUNT NUMBER XXXXXXXXXXX
THIS ITEM HAS BEEN DELETED

ACCOUNT NAME – ACCOUNT NUMBER XXXXXXXXXXX
THIS ACCOUNT IS STILL BEING INVESTIGATED

Explanation of Reinvestigation Results

When reinvestigating disputed information, CSC procedure is to contact the source of the information request directly either by an automated system, by letter, or by telephone. Upon receipt of your request, we will provide you with the company name and the address of the source contacted. In addition, a telephone number will be provided when available.

If the results of the reinvestigation indicate that the source continues to report the information you disputed, you have the right to contact the creditor directly or request us to include a notation regarding the disputed information. You may also submit a brief statement to CSC that will be included at the end of all subsequent credit reports, which may serve as an explanation of any information you dispute.

Please note if the reinvestigation results in changing or deleting the information, you may request an updated credit report be sent to any credit grantor that received your credit report in the past six months, and any company which received your report for employment purposes.

Thank you for giving CSC the opportunity to serve you.

CHAPTER 5

Conclusion

CREDIT PLAYS A very important role in our society today. The writers and collaborators of this book have come together to paint the most clear and accurate picture of exactly how to repair a consumer's credit. Many research hours and days went into this journey. Credit can be a consumer's best friend one day and then the worst nightmare the next.

There are many ways to protect your credit, and one of the most important ways is credit monitoring – this ensures the credit bureau will contact you, the owner of the report, anytime someone applies for credit in your name. The process allows you to be contacted, thus stopping fraud from occurring on your credit report.

The next best way to stop bad credit is strict discipline. By employing the process of discipline, the consumer can carefully review each item they need to purchase, carefully analyze the amount they have to spend and the bills they owe, and then make a sound and timely decision on what and when to buy goods on credit. Cash is a great weapon against buying on credit.

This book was a journey into credit/debt management and credit repair. The authors' intentions are to give to the public the necessary tools in order to maintain, clean, and safeguard the credit report. The samples used in the manual are meant to guide the consumer through each of the phases of credit repair and to assist with each step. The models shown may not be the exact format of what you will receive, as they vary from state to state and agency to agency; however, they are similar to the correspondence you can expect. Best of luck on your journey, and remember, good credit is only six steps away.

EPILOGUE

Credit Facts and Figures

How your score affects your mortgage rate for a $300,000 30-year fixed-rate loan		
FICO score	APR	**Monthly payment**
760-850	5.860%	$1,772
700-759	6.082%	$1,814
660-699	6.366%	$1,870
620-659	7.176%	$2,031
580-619	8.820%	$2,375
500-579	9.679%	**$2,562**

Source: myFICO.com, rates as of May 7, 2007

How your score affects your auto loan rate for a $25,000 36-month auto loan		
FICO score	APR	**Monthly payment**
720-850	7.115%	$773
690-719	7.934%	$783
660-689	9.404%	$800
620-659	10.960%	$818
590-619	14.404%	$859
500-589	15.020%	

GLOSSARY

CREDIT SCORE (BEACON) – *is a number typically between 300 and 850, based on a statistical analysis of a person's credit files, to represent the creditworthiness of that person, which is the likelihood that the person will pay his or her bills. Using mathematical models, the FICO score takes into account various factors in each of these five areas: payment history, current level of indebtedness, types of credit used, and length of credit history and new credit in determining credit risk.*

CREDIT RATING – *assesses the credit worthiness of an individual, corporation, or even a country. It means an assessment of the worthiness of individuals and corporations. It is based upon the history of borrowing and repayment, as well as the availability of assets and extent of liabilities.*

CREDIT BUREAUS – *is a company that provides credit information on individual borrowers. This helps lenders assess credit worthiness, the ability to pay back a loan, and can affect the interest rate applied to loans.*

CREDIT REPAIR – *is the legal activity of correcting errors contained on any or all of the three consumer credit bureaus – TransUnion, Equifax, and Experian – which warehouse consumer credit information.*

The highly complex nature of storing every American citizen's credit history over the course of no less than ten to twelve years leaves much room for mistakes, errors, and even false information.

Credit fixing has been made easier for the average consumer and more difficult to sell as a service because of federal regulations.

Typically, any consumer who writes a letter disputing any inaccurate information can expect to have such information deleted from their credit bureau after having sent two such disputes by mail or over the Internet.

JUDGMENT – in a legal context, is synonymous with the formal decision made by a court following a lawsuit.

BAD DEBT – is the portion of receivables that can no longer be collected, typically from accounts receivable or loans.

CHARGE-OFF – is a debt that is deemed uncollectible by the reporting firm and is subsequently written off to bad debt.

CREDIT MONITORING – is the monitoring of your credit report in order to detect any suspicious activity or change in your credit report.

CREDIT REPORT – is, in many countries, a record of an individual's or a company's past borrowing and repaying, including information about late payments and bankruptcy. When a customer fills out an application for credit from a bank, store, or credit card company, his or her information is forwarded to a credit bureau, along with constant updates on the status of his or her credit accounts, address, or any other changes made since the last time he or she applied for any credit.

CREDIT INQUIRIES – inquires into applicant's credit history (number and type of inquiries into applicant's report).

CREDIT LIMIT – refers to the maximum amount of credit a bank or other lender will extend to a debtor, or the maximum that a credit card company will allow a cardholder to borrow on a single card.

Credit card companies will also allow you to change your credit limit, or limit the credit available to authorized users on the account. This is especially useful if you give your children an emergency card with, say, a low limit like $100.

Credit card limits are frequently raised when you continue paying on time and in full. You can usually request a credit limit increase from your card company as well.

CREDIT INVESTIGATION – provides information about the credit history and credit rating of the person or business you are searching. It will also give you some information about outstanding loan or credit card payments, if the borrower makes payments on time, if there are outstanding liens, and will help you to determine the level of risk involved in giving credit to the customer.

LATE PAYMENT – are payments received after the due date of the actual invoice.

ABOUT THE AUTHOR(S)

THE SMITH GROUP is an amalgamation of senior credit managers and financial analysts, certified in the area of credit analysis and credit management and repair. The group, based in Houston, Texas, has twenty-plus years of international as well as domestic credit experience.

Look for more self-help manuals coming soon from the Smith Group (TSG), such as "Ten Steps to Financial Freedom," "How to Invest with Confidence with Little or No Money," and "Ten Steps to Beautiful Hair."

REFERENCE

Wikipedia, credit score, 2006
http://en.wikipedia.org/wiki/Credit_fixing

Wikipedia, credit rating agency, 2006

Wikipedia, 2006 Credit
http://www.creditreport.com/index14m-dark15-off1.asp?src=ADSNR17843&cid
      =103&tid=11336058&kwd=txlk14
http://www.freecreditreport.com/Default.aspx?sc=667704&bcd=efcr29

WORD SEARCH

```
C H A R G E O F F J A X I Y
X R B H Y D C S P U Q R W R
V A E W N X G K V D S Q I D
P T A D L L A T E G X A N E
R I C X I Y E R Q E C R Q C
S N O B M T C F P M V L U V
U G N L I E A I U E B D I E
A Q B M T C R P O N M Z R V
E Z H L W D I X Y T D O I D
R T B E D D A B L K C R E T
U J C L F V P C H S P W S H
B K P A Y M E N T M L E R Q
G D L X C Y R E W V B A U Z
G N I R O T I N O M Q T Y W
```

CREDIT   CHARGE-OFF
RATING   INQUIRIES
BEACON   LATE
BUREAUS   PAYMENT
REPAIR   JUDGEMENT
MONITORING   SCORE
BADDEBT   LIMIT

INDEX